AMAZING ASIAN AMERICANS

Amazing Asian Americans

Astronaut Kalpana Chawla,
Reaching for the Stars

by
Ai-Ling Louie

Illustrated by
H. Rick Pettway

Astronaut Kalpana Chawla, Reaching for the Stars: Amazing Asian Americans

To Benjamin—A.L.
To my amazing grandson Mason—R.P.

Copyright ©2014 by Ai-Ling Louie. All rights reserved. No part of this publication may be reproduced, stored in a retrievable system or transmitted in any form or by any means, electronic, mechanical, photocopying, recording or otherwise without the prior written permission of the copyright holder, except brief quotations in a review.

Illustrations ©2014 by H.Rick Pettway

Designed by Jonathan Louie
Printed on Cover, 260 gsm C1S Artcard; Text, IVO 100gsm woodfree paper
ISBN-978-0-978746513
Library of Congress Control Number: 2013933337
Published by Dragoneagle Press
Box 30856
Bethesda, MD 20824 U.S.A.
Dragoneagle.com

Published 2014
First paperback printing March 2014

Publisher's Cataloging-in-Publication Data
Louie, Ai-Ling. 1949-
    Astronaut Kalpana Chawla, Reaching for the Stars; Amazing Asian Americans
    by Ai-Ling Louie
    Illustrations by H.Rick Pettway
    Series: Amazing Asian Americans
    Summary. Juvenile biography of a South Asian American who became an American astronaut. Kalpana Chawla was born in India and emigrated to Texas to study aerospace engineering. Onboard the Space Shuttle Colombia, she became the first Asian American woman in space. Includes notes, references, children's bibliography and websites.
    ISBN 978-0-978746513
    1.Chawla, Kalpana. 1961-2003 – Juvenile Literature
    3. Astronauts—United States—Biography—Juvenile Literature
    4. Asian Americans—Biography—Juvenile Literature
    5. Women—Biography
    5. Columbia (Space Shuttle)
    6. Space Flight
    I. Pettway, H.Rick

2014
629.4

Manufactured in Hong Kong by Regal Printing Limited
Photo Credits: back flap, [top, Melanie Prange; bottom, Deborah Pettway],
p. 47 NASA, p. 48 iStock

Astronaut Kalpana Chawla
Reaching for the Stars

Amazing Asian Americans

by Ai-Ling Louie
illustrated by H. Rick Pettway

dragoneagle press

The little girl with the big eyes held her sister's hand. They had come to the principal's office to enroll the girl in nursery school. The principal said, "What is her name?"

"At home we call her Montu, but that's just her baby name. We were thinking of Kalpana or Sunaya."

The small girl hid her face in her sister's dress.

The principal smiled and asked, "And Montu, what name do you like?"

"Kalpana," she replied clearly and without a moment's hesitation.

Kalpana was the youngest of four children. She grew up in the small town of Karnal in India. Kalpana's family was wealthy. Her father owned a tire factory. One steamy, uncomfortably hot night the entire Chawla family took sleeping mats to the roof. The sky was deep blue and millions of stars sent their greetings to Kalpana in sparkling light. She didn't want to close her eyes and miss a single one. But she knew she must rest, because she had asked her brother Romi to ride bikes with her to the Air Club. Tomorrow was the big day.

A Pushpak airplane glided closer and closer to the runway. Its engines grew louder. And then, bouncing once, it was on the ground, and the brakes went "she-e-e-e" as they strained to slow the little plane. Kalpana watched open-mouthed. She told her brother, "Someday that's going to be me."

Kalpana was a girl who liked to wear pants. She would only wear a sari for Indian dancing or for weddings. She did well in school. Judo was her favorite sport. She loved throwing boys.

She always seemed to know what she wanted. One day when she was applying for a school, a teacher told her, "No, you can't study airplanes. That's only for boys."

Kalpana said, "Well, I don't think so. Put me down for aerospace engineering."

Mama liked the determined independent streak in her youngest child. When Mama wasn't busy taking care of Grandmother or visiting the Sikh temple, she spent time with her daughter.¹ She encouraged Kalpana to follow in the path of her sisters and go to college. Mama was delighted when Kalpana, the only girl studying aerospace engineering, came in third in the class, beating out all but two of the boys.

But when it came time to leave the family to continue her studies, it was her father she had to convince. Papa looked deep into her eyes and said, "Are you sure you don't want to stay here, get married, and have children?"

"I know what I'm doing, Papa-ji. Please, it's all I've ever dreamed of."

Soon she was packing her bags. She took her first long airplane flight halfway across the world to the United States and the University of Texas at Arlington. There she began to spend long hours doing experiments and working on equations. To earn money she helped students learn math and science. She was a good teacher. Kalpana had learned English when she was in grade school and spoke it with a slight British accent.[2]

Living in the apartment down the hall from Kalpana was a man named Jean-Pierre Harrison who was studying to be a pilot. When Jean-Pierre found out why Kalpana had come to Texas, he invited her to go flying with him. He took her up in a Piper Cub on one of his exercises.

Kalpana loved flying in the small two-seater. She wasn't afraid when the ground tilted this way or that,

and she loved the freedom of seeing nothing before her but open sky. Someday she was going to learn to be a pilot, but now she was too busy with her studies. She wanted to get the most education possible and get her doctorate in aerospace engineering.

Kalpana kept herself very busy, but she wasn't too busy to fall in love. One year after they met, Kalpana and Jean-Pierre were married. They both knew so much about airplanes that they often spoke like this:

Jean-Pierre pointed at the sky and said, "What kind of plane is that?"

"A Boeing 727."

"Ah, but what model?"

Kalpana hesitated and then playfully punched her husband's arm, saying, "You can't possibly know from here. You're just teasing me."

Kalpana's father took a while to get used to the fact that his new son-in-law was not Indian. Kalpana was afraid to tell her father, and so he was the last in the family to know. Papa-ji went to his room in his house and stayed there for a week, not talking to anyone. Then he walked out, and he seemed to have made up his mind, because after that he started treating Jean-Pierre as one of the family.

Mama was pleased that Kalpana and Jean-Pierre were married. The young couple was living in Colorado when Mama came for a long visit. Jean-Pierre, who now had his pilot's license, flew Kalpana and Mama in a private jet to some of the most beautiful parks in the West.

Kalpana and Mama walked arm-in-arm, marveling at the red rocks nature had carved. Kalpana loved everything about Bryce Canyon National Park and didn't want to leave.

"Watch out!" Jean-Pierre warned. "There's an ant crossing the trail."

Kalpana laughed and gave him a playful swat and said, "He's making fun of us for being vegetarian." Kalpana did not consider herself to be a religious Sikh, but she did keep her family's customs of not eating meat and avoiding hurting animals.

While in Colorado, Kalpana began to train to be a pilot. On the weekends she would go to a nearby airport to take lessons. She decided not to be Jean-Pierre's pupil and took another teacher. Kalpana even joined a flying club for women. She enjoyed the trips the club took together. At home, she told her husband

she thought she was a better pilot than any of the other women. Gliders also interested her. Gliders had no engines. They rode the air currents. Kalpana loved flying gliders. One time she accidentally landed one on its nose. Luckily, she wasn't hurt.

One day Kalpana saw an ad. It said, "Become an astronaut. NASA has openings."³ Kalpana's heart skipped a beat. To be an astronaut and go up hundreds of miles with a thundering rocket—that was the ultimate best for any flight buff.

1. A candidate had to be a pilot or a scientist. (Kalpana had graduated from the University of Colorado at Boulder with her doctorate in aerospace engineering.)
2. in excellent health. (That was Kalpana for sure! She kept herself slim and fit.)
3. between sixty-two and seventy-five inches tall. (She just made it at sixty-two inches.)
4. an American citizen. (Kalpana had lived in this country for twelve years. As much as she loved India, it was America that had given her the opportunity to be who she wanted to be. She had taken her oath as an American in 1991.)

The first time she applied to the astronaut program, she didn't get in. But in 1994 she got the magic phone call. The director of astronaut training asked, "Do you still want to come work for us?" What a silly question!

Kalpana felt like the luckiest person in the world! She would be training to be one of the seven astronauts aboard the space shuttle, travelling around the earth at speeds of seventeen thousand miles an hour.[4]

When she met the other astronaut trainees, she was her usual soft-spoken self. Soon though, she began to speak up, especially when others raised questions. There were a lot of different kinds of training to be done.

One of them had the class jumping out of airplanes and parachuting to the ground. One of her classmates said, "Is it really necessary to—" Kalpana began to answer but he cut her off with, "Give me a break— you can't know everything!"

Kalpana went home angry and hurt. She told her husband what had happened. He said, "It's because he's a hot-shot military pilot, and not a scientist like you. And remember, you have to learn to live together in that cramped spaceship for two weeks."

"Don't you think I know that?" she said. What was she supposed to do—cover up all she knew? As for living and working together, she was well aware that astronauts have to work as a team.

Finally, it was November 19, 1997, the day of the launch. The astronauts boarded the Space Shuttle Columbia for flight STS-87 and took off in a streak of flame. Once in orbit, they began to prepare for their main tasks. Kalpana's was to use the robot arm to move the SPARTAN satellite from the hold of the space shuttle and ready it for release. SPARTAN was a six-million dollar piece of equipment built to make measurements of the sun. Kalpana slowly moved the gold-wrapped satellite a safe distance from the shuttle. Kalpana was finally ready. "And launch!" she said as she let it go. Everybody stared. The satellite was not moving. No thrusters were firing. Kalpana moved the robot arm to grab the satellite for another try. Accidentally, she knocked the satellite with the arm and the satellite began to spin dangerously. Astronauts Scott and Doi had to suit up and go out on a spacewalk to recapture the SPARTAN. It was decided the satellite would have to be brought back to earth.

Reporters asked Kalpana what had gone wrong. She admitted it was her fault. She had missed a step in the launch procedure and the satellite had failed to start as it was supposed to. After many months, a NASA study cleared Kalpana of any blame. It said there should have been a way for the crew to check to see if the satellite were ready for launch. Still, Kalpana knew she had made a terrible error.

Everybody makes mistakes; it's only human. But it must have been especially hard for Kalpana. She said, "…everybody was pointing fingers at me." [5]

Kalpana was a proud, highly accomplished professional, and it was painful to be known as the astronaut who, when the eyes of the world were watching, made the six-million-dollar mistake.

Kalpana kept working at NASA, hoping to get another chance to fly. Six long years later she was overjoyed to be aboard Columbia for STS-107.

It was day thirteen of the sixteen day flight. An experiment was supposed to begin. It was to test how much mist (water droplets floating in air) was needed to put out a fire. This could help save lives. When it didn't work properly, Astronaut Mike Anderson figured out there was a loose connection in one of the lines. The entire machine would have to be taken apart to reach a tube, and then the machinery had to be put back together again. The only problem was the astronauts were on a tight schedule. No one had any time to spare.

"I'll do it!" Kalpana said. She volunteered to give up one of only two rest periods she was allowed during the sixteen day flight. She worked through lunch and would only stop when she was required to sleep. Following her example, other astronauts began to give up their rest periods too. They worked all day on the mist experiment with no time off, but they got the job done. Thirty-two of the planned thirty-four runs were completed before the astronauts had to stop and prepare for reentry.

The results were relayed back to the nervous scientists on earth. Cheering broke out when they saw the numbers start coming in. The scientists were overjoyed and grateful to Kalpana for saving the day.

Hearing this put Kalpana on top of the world! She had shown everyone she had learned her lesson. She was no longer the "know-it-all" who made the big mistake. She was now seen as a fine astronaut, a well-respected scientist, and a team leader, and that is how she wanted to be remembered.

As all this was happening inside the Columbia, there was a dangerous situation on the outside of the vehicle. The astronauts didn't know that Columbia had a hole in her heat shield. It had been caused by flying debris during takeoff. Shortly after reentry to the Earth's atmosphere, one of the Shuttle's wings heated to dangerous levels and broke off. It was a great tragedy and sadly none of the astronauts survived.⁶

Kalpana Chawla is an American hero. She accomplished so much in her forty-one years. She was the first Asian American woman in space. She travelled thirty-one days, fourteen hours, fifty-four minutes in the shuttle, orbiting the earth fifty-two times. She is at rest now. Her ashes are spread, just as she wanted them, among the red rocks she loved in Utah.

The United States mourned the loss of the astronauts. At the White House, President George W. Bush gave the grieving Papa-ji a hug. India named a planetarium and a medical college after Kalpana. In Karnal, the Chawla family established a free math and science school for young women. Jean-Pierre wrote a book celebrating her life. Brother Romi said something very heartfelt: "To me my sister is not dead. She is immortal. Isn't that what a star is? She is a permanent star in the sky. She will always be up there where she belongs."[7]

NOTES

[1] Sikhism, pronounced "SĬK ism", is a religion founded in India. It is not Muslim or Hindu. The men often wear turbans.

[2] The English ruled India from 1848 to 1947.

[3] NASA stands for National Aeronautics and Space Administration, a part of the US government.

[4] The space shuttle was an American vehicle designed to take off like a rocket, orbit the earth, and land like an airplane. Six shuttles were built. They flew from 1981 to 2011.

[5] Chien, Philip. (2006) *Columbia Final Voyage*. NY, Copernicus Books, p. 54.

[6] Columbia broke up over Texas on February 1, 2003. On board were Rick Husband, Commander; Willie McCool, Pilot; Dave Brown, Mission Specialist; Kalpana Chawla, Mission Specialist; Mike Anderson, Payload Commander; Ilan Ramon, Payload Specialist.

[7] From "A Muse for Indian Women". February 2, 2003. *The Los Angeles Times*. Timeline

SELECTED REFERENCES

Cabbage, Michael and Harwood, William. (2004) *Comm Check… The Final Flight of the Columbia*. New York, Free Press/ Simon and Schuster

Harrison, Jean-Pierre. (2011) *The Edge of Time, The Authoritative Biography of Kalpana Chawla*. Los Gatos, CA, Harrison Publishing

Wallack, William. ed. (2012) *Celebrating Thirty Years, The Space Shuttle Program*. Washington, DC, U.S. Government Printing Office

CHILDREN'S BIBLIOGRAPHY AND WEBSITES

Kaur-Singh, Kanwaljit. (2007) *My Sikh Faith, My Faith*. Mankato, MI, Cherrytree Books. Grades K-3

Ride, Sally and Okie, Susan. (1991) *To Space and Back, U.S. Astronaut Sally Ride Shares the Adventure of Outer Space*. New York, Beech Tree Books. Grades 3-6

Salawi, Dilip. (2004) *Kalpana Chawla, India's First Woman Astronaut*. New Delhi, India, Rupa and Co. Grades 3-6

Singh, Rina. (2011) Guru Nanak, *The First Sikh Guru*. Toronto, Canada, Groundwood Books. Grades 3-6

Stine, Megan. (2013) *Who Was Sally Ride?* NY, Grosset & Dunlap

Zuehlke, Jeffrey. (2007) *The Space Shuttle, Pull-Ahead Books*. Minneapolis, MN, Lerner Books. Grades K-3

- http://www.nasa.gov/audience/forkids/kidsclub/flash/index.html
- http://www.nasa.gov/audience/foreducators/index.html
- http://www.nasa.gov/audience/forstudents/k-4/index.html
- http://www.nasa.gov/audience/forstudents/5-8/index.html

Astronauts of the Space Shuttle Columbia, flight STS-107

pilot William McCool   *mission specialist* Michael Anderson
mission specialist David Brown   *Israeli payload specialist* Ilan Ramon
mission specialist Kalpana Chawla   *mission specialist* Laurel Clark
commander Rick Husband

AMAZING ASIAN AMERICANS

Amazing Asian Americans,
a series for the elementary school child.

Books in this series:
Vera Wang, Queen of Fashion
Yo-Yo and Yeou-Cheng Ma, Finding Their Way

To purchase copies visit our website:
dragoneagle.com

Coming next:
Patsy Takemoto Mink Fights for Equality